Rathsastr

Rathsastr

รัฐศาสตร์ (rathsastr)—"political science"

Sally Kendall

RESOURCE *Publications* • Eugene, Oregon

RATHSASTR

Resource Publications
An Imprint of Wipf and Stock Publishers
199 W. 8th Ave., Suite 3
Eugene, OR 97401

www.wipfandstock.com

PAPERBACK ISBN: 978-1-7252-9344-1
HARDCOVER ISBN: 978-1-7252-9345-8
EBOOK ISBN: 978-1-7252-9346-5

04/12/21

Contents

disease

When I was a Child

When I was a child
She poured hot glue on my face
It wasn't on purpose
She thought she was supposed to
That it was best
I guess that's what you're supposed to do when your face itches

She put these lovely glasses on my face
Full of roses in the shade
With pink and red and floral green
The kind the cool kids get from the mall

She told me they would help me see
That the itch doesn't just go away
And that I needed my parents to adjust it

Well, I knew I would be in big trouble
About why I had glue on my face
And sure enough
I got the 3rd degree
I was banned from that teacher and places I would see her
It wasn't something I was supposed to bring up even
I even had to talk to the principal

But somehow they couldn't see my glasses
They were invisible?
But I saw roses
They were so beautiful
And I have spent my lifetime
Trying to take these hot glue glasses off my face
Because I'm not sure I know how to see without them

Coronavirus

There are things in life you can't control
Like this coronavirus
Spreading and
Destroying people's lives

But it's outside your hands
(hopefully)
Either that or you've got the virus
Because you don't want that on your hands

What do you do with those things you can't control
It's those A-words
Allowing
Acceptance
Identify the site picture
This is what we can do
This is what we can't
And this
This is what is
What they call
the present
But take a good look at the picture
Because you might miss something if you look in the wrong place

Maybe we needed the virus
To remind us that we are human
And our time is temporary

Maybe He allowed it to remind us
We are not in control
And what do you do about those things you can't control?

You put those in His hands
And then you do those things you CAN do

Pestilence

In her room
There was a mask
The kind the witch doctors wear
To keep them from the plague
From the pestilence

"He who desires but acts not, breeds pestilence."

"Eternity is in love with the productions of time."

William Blake

Passover

In a faraway place
In another time
My people were in captivity
And My heartbeat was to set them free
Teach the masters of slavery

So I sent Egypt deadly plagues:
Turned water to blood
Frogs and boils
Flies and hail
Disease and darkness
All the pestilence
Locusts to crawl across the land
And took the firstborns from their hand

Only did the angel pass
The houses mark-ed by the lamb
Whose blood was spread acrost the posts
Yes, the sacrificial Lamb
Telling of the Christ, I AM
Remember then the great

Passover
Reminder
Kept in
Jewish Seder

The land was full of
Lamentations

Told Pharaoh
LET MY PEOPLE GO
I split the sea to set them free
So they'd return to worship Me

That they might know
I AM THE LORD

Exodus 7–12

Sonnet

I found you in the words that lined the page
Expressions from whence admirations pulse
A book that traps me in a fit of rage
Of longings that her other might repulse
I shut the book and pondered at the thing
Yet nothing on my shelves could quite explain
For what and how and why the heart doth sing
But only human error and disdain
For love a man's religion might divide
Creating groups of factions and of sects
Who is to say that love's not borne of pride
Or still perhaps of passions gone unchecked
And so I'll ask my Lord then once again
What purpose would He use my love for then

Mirror

I looked at you
I saw a mirror
Of hurts of fears of scars of tears
Memories of joy and pain
Reminding me I felt the same

Things I thought that I'd worked out
In the background
That old wallpaper
Underneath

I thought that I had let you go
But I was hoping at least
At least
You might have mixed feelings
I know you do
If you were honest you'd know that too

I know you felt betrayed by me
But I didn't mean you harm
I was trying to be honest with myself
The same way you didn't mean me harm

I loved the time I shared with you
You gave me the canvas to display my art
You gave me something tangible to all my missing feelings
And I guess at the end of the day

As there are many ways to express or display it
Though there might have been great debate at what was loving
    and what was not
The simple truth of the matter was—
I loved you

And today
Today I love you
By respecting where you are
And reminding myself not to take it personal
And maybe
Maybe you loved me too
In the way you knew how
And maybe . . . maybe you have mixed feelings

Falling Upwards

I fell down the stairs once
Grabbed the railing for dear life while my feet went out from
    under me

Then, the way a ray of light and angel appears in the movies
I heard a voice from up above
And I realized
You were at the top of the stairs
Too high for me to reach

So there I was
Dazed in a wonder
Falling upwards

Your Picture

The thing that shook me about your picture
Was I saw your features had changed
The softness in your face
The look of nurturing
The mother you had become

It was like
I had missed out on when it happened
The you I knew had become someone else
Though she was still you

The picture reminded me of that softness I felt
The gentleness in your cheeks
Whispering at my tender heart strings
Reminding me
How much love I felt for you

You looked happy
When he told me the words you spoke
It sounded like you
And my heart yearned
At your picture, worth thousands of words

Jewelry Store

Tonight, I walked past a jewelry store
With flashes of sterling silver in the window
One was a little cat sitting on a sliver of the moon
And I remembered
I remembered all those cat things I had sent you
I thought of how those gifts made me feel close to you
When you were not close by
Having something to send you-
This brought you to me
In that tangible way
It's like a piece of my heart wrapped up in those gifts

If I'm not careful I might
Buy the entire store

So tonight when I had the idea of someone new to buy those
    necklaces for

I remembered you
And it would be hard for any to compare
With how much of my heart belonged to you

Complexity

Tell me of complexity
The things I saw but couldn't speak
The things that words could not quite capture
Exquisite bliss
Imposing rapture
Resplendent
Opulent
And pure
The holy grail
The wanted cure
Brilliance I could not describe
Imperial as the changing tide

Queen of Clubs

I saw the Queen of Clubs
Had a soft look in her eye
Like she had witnessed just too much
Like her vineyard grapes were crushed

There in silent contemplation
She gripped the yellow fleur
From the fields now in her hand
She gazed across the barren land

Scattered near and spread out far
Measly peasants farmed the ground
Tilled the land and labored long
So the dirge became their song

I saw the Queen of Clubs
A wistful longing in her eye
She dropped the scepter by her side
She had drunk formaldehyde

A Whole Half

There's a whole half of me
That didn't get to come here
That didn't get this education
That didn't have these luxuries
That didn't have this freedom

There's a whole half of me
That never had this opportunity
That never heard of what you're saying
That never had the funds
That never knew it was possible

There's a whole half of me
That wasn't caught up in the market
That wasn't concerned with leisure
That wasn't free to speak
That wasn't climbing the ladder

There's a whole half of me
That was happy with a little
That was happy just to labor
That was happy for them all
That was happy

Empath

Being an empath
Has its burdens
I can sense you
Before I want to
Before I'm even trying
I can hear the music
From far far away
And I can tell you how this constellation works

While you all walk by one another as individuals
The same way some of you can
Each sensing a different element
In the electric blue of this spiderweb
This century we are running through
Together

I can tell you what I feel
See the injustices you have suffered
Beneath your gangly walk
Your face pleaded all your pains
The life you had witnessed
The tears no one saw
Finite in time
On this slippery timeline
While what has gone before
Is lost beneath your feet
The past mixed up in this present
Reverberating

Real Estate

Nothing in my heart could be quite so large as the space you've
    taken up
In fact, there's not even room to squish by
All I can see is stacks and piles of
Love poems and gifts
Memories
Clothes
There's barely room to squeeze through
Every pulsing thought of you
My love for you is large
And you've got quite the piece of real estate

Off the Internet

When I move off the internet
I can feel the distance
Just how many miles
How many stoplights
How many highways
I am away from you

Granted, it's closer than the other country
But you are still far
Like out of reach
And I'm wandering the streets
Towards your house
Towards your driveway

I've never been to your house
But I've dreamed of it
Many times
I've sat at your kitchen table
I've walked down the hallway
Enamored by what's on the wall

You're with your family
Where you belong
You're home
You're in a good place
And my heart is happy for you
But, alas ~ missing

I Said Goodbye

I said goodbye
But
You were really just in my backyard

All the little ones went to sleep

Some pulled out their laptops
Some pulled out their cards
Others the Xbox
Or clorox
Some their book for the evening
Some their drink before the night sky
Some in their N95 mask
Some typing the paper for their class
Some searching the menu of the sushi-go
Some stopping at the Daiso

I said goodbye
But I smiled
Because
I remembered object permanence
From attachment theory

And that you were just in the backyard

And when the sun comes up tomorrow
I'll find you on the journey as we move through this century

Half

I never should have needed to love you
But
I didn't see the full picture
I saw your other half
And not what I couldn't see
I don't know why my heart pounded so hard
The way a hammer meets a nail
With striking force

Crush

Hello Crush
Boy you are looking fancy today
You've got your song lighting up the sky
It's bright
It's hopeful
It's alive
In the best way something's ever been alive
You're wearing all the colors
Punk rock bracelets
Beats headphones rocking
Daydream by the Aces
Head up in the clouds

Crush! You are killing it!
Stop making the sky so d*mn beautiful!

Crush
Stop tickling me all over
I know you're taken
I know you're off-limits
For every reason in the world
Crush
I must be putting pressure on you
I know how to adore you from afar
I told you I had my glasses on
And they are rocking me in this whole new world
A whole new world

Sometimes
Looking over the cliff is
Insatiably attractive
Dangerously exciting
Impossibly alluring
And while I know I would lose my life
There is something magnificent
To look into the beauty of the depths
Until I'm hung up on a fucking satellite

Lust

Lust is selfish
It doesn't truly consider others
Doesn't consider their job
Doesn't consider perception
Doesn't consider what they care about
Doesn't consider what's honorable
Doesn't consider marriage
Doesn't consider reality
Doesn't consider
It's wrapped up in itself
In fulfilling oneself
Wrapped up in a lie
Lies are attractive
The Truth is not so attractive
The Truth is ugly
The Truth exposes imperfections
The Truth sees us as we are
The Truth knows all angles
The Truth is separate from darkness
The Truth is Jesus Christ
The Truth sets us free

Gave Them Over

We use what's wicked
To press against the
Truth
To cover what is plain
The truth of God in plain sight
What which is
Invisible
He made clear
Take a look at what's been made
Eternal power
Divine nature
People are without excuse

Futile thoughts
Deceitful heart
Considered smart
But quite converse
Foolishly took the reverse
Glory that was meant for God
Exchanged for crawling images

So God gave them over
To sinful desires
Truth for lies
Worshipping creatures
Not the Creator

So God gave them over
To shameful lusts
For what is unnatural
Inflamed and
Acting shamefully
Their error bearing penalty

So God gave them over
To a corrupt mind
Full of depravity
Pride
Infidelity
No understanding
No love and
No mercy
Knowing God's law
But supporting the lawless

Romans 1

threat

The Bandwagon

Did you know
That day I knocked on your door
I was so brave
It was like
Diplomacy in action
Between warring states

Except peace could not be attained
You were not open to negotiations
Balancing power
Balancing threat
And I was hanging in the balance

As time went on
As worlds evolved
I was left in the ether
Stuck in the airspace
In No Man's Land

You took the easy way out
Jumped on the bandwagon
And didn't take me with you
So I was left alone
One of those little states
With no power

So I'll tell you why power attracts
It promises protection, belonging
Secure attachment
That you're worth fighting for
To fight for you in times of war

Alliances

The door knocking—
It's making alliances
Share with me some of your power
Because we're in this together
And I need you to survive

Except now
Now I can tell you need me
You want to re-negotiate
Well
I am caught up in the bitterness
Of all that has past
Because it was bitter

Force Field

I'm rolling down the street
In a giant field of force
Electric purple, orange, clear
With a sparkling, risky steer!

Let the Hi-jet hit my side
I'll bounce right up into the sky
I've got Jesus at the center
He'll tell me who can enter

Careful when you touch my force field
There's an electric shock I have to turn off first

Risk Averse

I have no
Membrane with the universe
Ask me if I'm risk averse
Tell me where I start and end
Space and time to hold my hand
Give me then a place to bleed
A place to soar a place I need
Take in all the information
All goes back to education
How to filter how to sort
How to unf*&# the false report

Purple Glass

I walked up to the force field
Invisible
A solid wall

Only certain elements could pass
Not mud not brick not steel not brass
Only permitted—purple glass

I reached within
And saw again
A force field
Where none could go
A wild typhoon
And tornado

The force field there that kept it in
Was made of fire
Electro-wire

See, purple glass
It's hard to find
It's cuts are deep
But meant to keep

So fall into the field of force
Learn the pathway
Find the course

Lost Stitch

How do you pick up that lost stitch
That was dropped way back there
Well
You might need someone to help you pull the thread
You might need to take that fabric in your hand
The fabric of the entire timeline
And shake it a little
See what stays
What falls apart
Uncover the deception
Make that effort counterproductive for the enemy
An iterative process
Strengthen the base

Fabric

Take the fabric of the timeline in your hand
Yank it
They might understand

The Past

The past can get blurry
All mixed up
Mixed into one
Too many ways to frame
So start from the beginning
The sequence of events
It helps you see through the clouds

Hiroshima

I CAN RUN TO HIROSHIMA
LIKE THAT
ALL THE WAY TO HIROSHIMA
LIKE THAT
WHEN I GET TO HIROSHIMA
THE PEOPLE THERE WILL SAY
I'M GONNA PUT YOU IN ROM
FOR FOURTEEN DAYS
OH YEAH
FEELING GOOD
ON A RUN
JUST FOR FUN

My Parents

My parents are from two nations
One that sports red white and blue
One of communist bamboo
A marriage of the market share
And partnership beyond the Scare

Secrets held between the two
Created rifts, distrust, the flu

Might this marriage fall apart
Ask your children where to start
Ask the man who married you
The One who designed marriage too

Political Asylum

Sanctuary, sanctuary!
Free me from their persecution
Protection found in sovereignty
Power dispels anxiety
Hide me underneath His rod
A place safeguarded there by God

Nationalism

I am the state
And I'm here to tell you what it means to be me
To tell you what I worship
And what I give my respects to
Give me the freedom to rule my own
Nationalism

Tell you where I plan to
Seize territory
If you are my ally
Where I'm pouring my funds
To build up my defense

I'll tell you of the grievances
If I trust you
And you might help me make reparations
We might hold them accountable
Win back lost ground
Fight for those that had no voice
And maybe I could help you also

I am the state
And I'm here to make conquest
Define, protect, assert my borders
Boundaries
And my members

Tell you of my interests
Though I want to hear yours also
Though you might be more powerful than me
Help me keep my sense of what is
Me
While my sights are set on Thee
A true nationalist

Love Unrequited

You seem like a safe person to be in love with
Let me clarify
Not the unrequited hopeless love kind of love
The expressed love
The kind where
You know it's good
Because it's a really good example
A really good example of the kind God is
The kind that comes from God
Who He's the original author of
And you are a living breathing picture of it
Reflecting Him
That's why it's so beautiful
It's a picture of God
And that would make sense, wouldn't it?
For love is from God
And everything that loves is born of God and knows God
He who loves not
Knows not God
For God is love

It would be great to end there
But if I think about it too long
It starts to turn into that
Hopeless kind of unrequited love
And then it starts to hurt

And bleed
And yearn
And ache
But don't let it go so far
It doesn't need to go that far
Be grateful
Appreciate what it is
Love in the way that's good for her
And good for you
Love in the way that respects others
Like her husband
Don't forget that
She loves him
Don't forget that
Respect the lines
You'll get her more fully if you respect the lines
And then go back to God
The One who made her

death

War

Move the pieces on the board
All the pawns
All the players
Roles defining all the layers

While you work your strategy
Consider what the outcomes see

Protect the things that matter
WAR
The ones that paint the precious core

Climb down from your ivory tower
Remember why you have your power

Territory to be taken
Make new weapons while you're shaken

Move the pieces on the board
All the pawns
All the players
The enemy hides off in the shadows
Force his way into the light
We're fighting for your soul tonight

Kitchen Sink

I woke up to an odor strong
Went on to the kitchen sink
Resentment clogged up in the drain
Creating friction, pressure, strain
Building up from the disdain

So naturally I plugged my nose
Garbage disposal here we go
Stuck in there like white on rice
The button there would not suffice
Oh pungent stench that smokes from vice

I took a knife and plunged it deep
The crud there you would not believe
Cutting all those pieces out
Aromas I could do without
Hurts and fears—what's that about?

I let the Draino sit for hours
Layers of memory and shame
This would require something more
More than the convenience store
Sink replacement? What a chore

So I gave up and called the man
He worked for hours and days and weeks
Months and years and decades
And needless to say
I had to let it go to move into a new house

Dark Art

Tonight I made an offering
Sent my dark art up in flames
Pictures, faces with no names

They were better off in the hands of the One who could recognize
    them

Goya

I found myself
A part of your circle
The Goya on your shelves of spice
Spoke you needed no advice
Passionate in all your claims
Allegiances one and the same
On issues that divide the world
The people who your hearts beat for
Their jobs and yes, their rights to choose
Not just the things that line the news
Stake your flag on where you'll die
You might become a butterfly

Burn

There's a bad smell when plastic burns
That's the way memories smell when they burn
It's so hot
It's melting
Colors blending
Blurring
Bending
Stop it while you can
Hold the memory in your hand
It might sear into your skin a little
Might leave a mark
An engraving
Become a part of you
I would tell you to bring the memory to the sink, so we could
    rinse and sort, but
Cold water ruins the picture

Scalpel

I'll let you
Do a little surgery
Take a scalpel to the skin
Carefully expose the sin
But find the blunt force trauma wound
What others passed and just assumed
I'll show you what is underneath
But please—please don't use your teeth

Torture

There's this word I keep seeing
Everywhere recently
And that's the word torture

Well, this is concerning
A torture therapist
People tortured for Christ
The torture of obsession
It is even quite an ugly looking word
Just like contort
A vicious thwart
Inflicting pain
Go ask my brain

Torture
Scorcher
Unannounced and feared departure

The anguish we call suffering
Forced into a line for hanging
Find some quiet in the clanging
Jesus tortured for my saving

Two Sisters

Two sisters held the bridge's ledge
Up high above the waters

One named Grief
And one, Depression
Near big brother, Introspection

Both in dresses with pink bows
Looked down at where the rowboat rows
They saw the great big world below
Those things that no one else might know

The trees, the boats, and fishermen,
A plane that flew past all of them
The mother while her children play
Construction workers near the bay

Depression saw their toil and pain
A downpour came of sudden rain
There she grabbed her sister's hand
Her heart was buried in the sand

Grief told her it wasn't true
There was no pain but just the hue
"IT'S NOT TRUE!" she spouted out
But no one seemed to hear her shout

They sat despondent on the bench
Big brother watched
His coat was drenched
He opened up a large umbrella
Deep thoughts ran through the lanky fellah

"Perhaps then we could make a deal."
Grief tried again—to no avail
Depression lifeless at the scene
The quiet there a false serene

Introspection stroked her hair
Remembering what the Wise man said
Of Vanity—to grasp for wind
How to accept this futile end?

Grief saw a pathway through the trees
A journey to acceptance sees
She shook her sister from her mope
To take her on the road to hope

Darkness and Missing

I had two visitors this evening
One was Darkness in his fortress of a robe
And the other
That little girl named
Missing
In the red cardigan sweater with holes

He had her by the hand
And he wasn't letting go

I had to fight with him to have you freed
It was the kind of battle that lit the night sky

I plunged right
And Darkness swept across my ground

Missing stood there
Brave
She knew it would pass

I took out my sword
That one I've practiced with
I took out those Truths
And I used every last one of them

Such that Darkness fled

I took Missing home
And we went for ice cream
And I cleaned my sword
READY

Across the way
I knew my Lord already WON
And He was coming

Pain

There's pain in the world
Unbearable suffering
We each find our way to shield ourselves from it
To hide from
What might cause it
To fill our lives with antidotes
With other things
To avoid, distract, perhaps even wallow

There's pain in the world
And it's awfully heavy
Reaching into the crevices
Finding ways to lodge
I can't seem to run away from it
She just morphs into another form

Pain, this bloody old widow in a dirty head covering
Elderly with wrinkles
With a darker shade like tan fruit leather
She needs someone to help her wherever she goes
Dependent
Fragile, weak, brittle

The bleeding woman who knows
If she can just touch the cloak of the Christ
She'll be healed
And hope propels her
Pushes her through the crowds
For the moment she might stumble into His presence
Only to find beyond her wildest dreams
There was POWER that would go out from Him

Transformative power
From this Man of Sorrows
Acquainted with Grief
Surely He has borne our sorrows
Stricken by God, afflicted
Despised, rejected, crushed, wounded
Pierced for our transgressions
All of my regressions
A Man of Grief
Oppressed
Anguished
Bearing the iniquity of us all

Holy Wrath

While Moses on Mount Sinai met with God
The people came to Aaron in complaint
Demanding he produce them a fascade
They tossed their rings of gold without restraint
With graving tool in hand, he carved a calf
There fixed before a shrine of offerings
So God sent Moses down on His behalf
His anger hot at wayward worshipping
For God delivered them from Egypt's hand
His fire consumed the idol left in dust
They drank the bitter water—His command
But sons of Levi made the Lord their trust
He sent the plague and blot them from His book
His holy wrath that day 3,000 took

Exodus 32

My Time Here is Short

My time here is short
So, I'm here at my planning table
Working the strategy
Identifying the objective
Finding where to start
Problem framing
Always with the problem framing

There's challenges and opportunities
Things I have not yet imagined
Knowledge I have not yet stumbled upon
Left turns only He knows

I'm charting the path
Reading the signs
Weaving through the peoples and
Quandries and passing fads
Reminding myself not to take it personal

I'm going after the goalposts
Following His instructions and design
Getting rid of excess
Giving Jesus my mess
My time here is short

Death

Death is like one of those fogs
That is off to the side, nearby
It's so close
But also so distant
Yet somehow
It creeps up
Suddenly
Alarmingly
Treacherously
In a swift
Noiseless way
Where there are no sounds
Only moments of last breaths

She is tricky
Rude
Deceitful
Hiding from the light
Cowering from who might expose her
Finding safety in the shadows
Waiting to be exposed

Death is like
The song that ends
Marveling at the piece it was
The meaning
And the purpose

And what parts of the song you shared
What all of it was meant for
What the song told you
What she sang to you and
And she showed you
(or corrected you on)
Who she was
Who she is
But now what she is to-be?
The to-be is here
She's in the to-be
What she is to-be
Cease to-be
New to-be

"Death is swallowed up in victory"
1 Corinthians 15:54–58

divine

Fine China

You and me
See, we are fine china
Mine is made of porcelain and jade
A fragile piece
A lucky trade
Yours was baked in Western sun
Hidden colors
A truly special edition
Theirs is of a thermos strong
Durable for what comes along
But you and me
See we can break
So find protection
In the quake

Home

Home was the bench outside your office
The hallway by your door
The parking lot before your building
The news that aired for your country

Home was the place I knew you loved and poured into
Because that's what I loved and poured into
Though I didn't really love it myself
I just loved you

Home was the world you lived in
Home was your airspace
Home was the private thoughts you shared with me

The bottom line was
Home was with you
And I couldn't get around this

Who I Am

Let me remind you
Who you are

Remember from a lifetime past
People in your constellation
The lines that touched
Can touch again

We met before the world was changed
And I saw you in the new world

You reminded me
Who I am

Solar System

I found you in the solar system
Near the stars out past the sun
Underneath the Saturn ring
Close to one of my heartstrings

Daylight burned while
Nighttime sang
Sweet Capricorn
Now lost in form

Find me when she comes around
Venus telling us of love
The lines that hold us all in place
Reaching into outer space

Find me in the present, now
In the moonlight—yes that's how
Showing me that I can feel
Reminding me that it was real

Little Kitty Calico

Little kitty calico
Down the street it's time to go
Follow Ashley all the way
Might even take you home today

Love

Love takes many forms
Travels down the street
Reaches high
Reaches low
Stoops in grace to all below

Love- it bends
Favor extends
Kindness I could never earn
Did not deserve
Begin to learn

Catch the gift in hand
Accept
That which those knelt down to bless
Let Him find you where you are
Close the distance, debonair
Invite you to His reservoir

Coffee

You reminded me of the first time she invited me for coffee

I can't tell you how terrified I was
All I remembered was there were little pigs in the glass table

I just remember I was so happy to finally have the chance to talk

She didn't know how many years I had been waiting

So, of course I sat outside her door
It was home

Metronome

Listen for the metronome's
Pulsing beat
Steady
Ready

Wait
She's going to set the rhythm
Fall in step
The timing set
A constant tempo
Slight rubato
Synchronize
The falling rise

Click
You'll hear
The simple tone
The metronome

She'll tell you when
Just wait for then
Be patient, friend

Timeline

You looked at me
I looked at you
And we watched time pass together
As we shared this portion of the timeline

You saw me in that moment
And you knew
Just like I saw you in that moment
And I knew
And I didn't need the words

We had what they call the "you and I" meeting
Where we came face to face
With a real conversation
Both spoken and silent
Against its backdrop of shame and fears
The things built up over the years

You looked at me
I looked at you
And we shared those moments in the timeline
Because God knows
Some burdens are too large for us to carry on our own

Miracle

There's the miracle of birth
And the tragedy of death
And the thing that leaves us wanting on either end of it

There's hello
And there's goodbye
And there's the part we spend in between

There's starting
And there's ending
And there's what we call unfinished

There's the you of then
And there's the you of now
All the same person He designed

He's the Alpha
And Omega
The Beginning and the End
The Constant through the change
The Rock inside the storm
The Strong Tower we run to
The One who waits to meet us
To remind us that He sees

New Wallpaper

A messenger came to me today
He informed me that it was time for remodeling
That we were stripping the wallpaper down
Putting up new surroundings
So that there could be
Full attention to Christ
The way Mary did it
While Martha asked her to help serve
And she just sat at his feet
To listen
Undistracted
Heart fully engaged
We're putting up some
New wallpaper
And it is quite exquisite
In the way that
Words cannot describe

Fruit

Fruit comes from the tree
Good fruit that is the best
Give that to the Lord
No one else rates
The fruit of all your labor
Put it in His hands
A smoking aroma to the One who made it all
Check the fruit on your tree
Is it ripe for the King
What is the song your heart might sing
Sing it only for the King

For sin is crouching at the door
Deception by the tree
By the one Christ was hanging on
Waiting patiently to overtake you
Asking for the best
To give the Christ the rest
Sin is crouching by your tree
Master then this enemy
Weed it out out of your garden
Remember the dear cost of pardon
But if you give it to Him first
He said He'll quench your thirst
Just as He did for the woman with five husbands

Drink then from His well
And watch your tree grow tall
Faith just like a mustard seed
Much different than a hollow reed
Keep her from the rocks and thorns
Close to the truth away from scorns
Sit by godly counsel, grow!
By your fruits the world will know
Protected by His watchful eye
The seed that grows she must first die
Planted there by flowing streams
Day and night wrapped in her dreams

Sanctuary

That place where it's just you and God
Before the open night sky
Under the moon
Where all is stripped away
And you're alone with Him
Where your longings are naked before Him
Your cares
Your worries
Your wounds
Your heartaches
Beneath the Master of the Universe
The Alpha and Omega
The Beginning and the End
Creator and Redeemer
Messiah King and Friend
Lover of my soul
King above all kings
All hail the power of Jesus' name
The Son of Man
Lamb who was slain
Lion of Judah none can tame

God Who Wrote

God who wrote
Love unrequited
Was indicted
Extradited

God who wrote
Love into time
Who called me Mine
Who was maligned

God who wrote
His heart for me
Penned history
Love mystery

God who wrote
His Holy Word
Like none have heard
Love transferred

God who wrote
Could not be bound
In glory crowned
Took lost to found

God who wrote
The antidote
The pathway back to
God who wrote

www.ingramcontent.com/pod-product-compliance
Lightning Source LLC
LaVergne TN
LVHW021615080426
835510LV00019B/2579